Co

ATOM BLAST

The murmur of soil and mortar
When the iron beast climbed down
A baby's toy lay abandoned
And the child had gone

Everyone was hiding silently
But why?
When the final, fatal blast subsided
Not one humble body could hope to be saved.

They shivered, they screamed, shook
And they screeched, but in vain
As the sphere descended filled with
Death.

To end their lonely misery
When the steel-solid touched the earth
One last whisper
One last solitary squeal
And the mountain germinated
With gases so hue-like
And pretty coloured
That they strangled the spirit
And form
Of those blood-filled
Sweating corpses
Plastered and buried their life
In caverns clawed up
By this gnawing finger
Of evil and symbolized
Power.

A baby's toy lay abandoned
And the child
Had gone.

Ann Zastawecki

ON THE BATTLEFIELD

We thought the living to be over there:
But now, we numbly stare
As corpses rise, and stretch, and walk,
And blankly talk
Of armistice, or guns.
Humankind! Who sent your sons
To shrink and wither, rot, away
From home? And why did they obey?

Because they understand the penalty
Of resistance and disloyalty?
The corpse that sags upon a tortured cross?
Six million corpses they saw tossed
Into the hideous pit, and burned?

What have we really learned?
That every body hurled into the grave
Left blood on mankind's hands. And have
We ever, for one second, paused
To think what really caused
Us to be here today, with tools
Of slaughter in the grasp of fools?

Chris Cotes

FACING

Facing of the enemy
Before beginning fire
Then we'll have explosion
Bodies fall on wire
Blood and guts is spilling
All over the field
Neither us nor enemy
Stop and say, 'We yield.'

Michael D Bedford

THE FRONT LINE

The tape was held,
As they single filed,
O'er no-man's-land,
Which death defiled,
While in their ears,
The deafening roar
Of firing shells
Crashed, evermore.

Mary McPhee

THE SUM

Opposing muddy trench
Pervading body stench
Artillery relentlessly pounds
Alarming deafening sounds
Men just in their prime
From the trench do climb
Distant ringing bell
Denies this living hell
Bodies stopping bullets
Blood flowing in rivulets
Shrapnel wounds horrific
From shelling unspecific
Tank grenade and gas
Still the troops amass
Generals in the rear
Show very little fear
To take another's life
In conflict or in strife
Bayonet bullet and bomb
Fuel this muddy maelstrom
Glory of this war
Lost in all the gore
Each country's awful truth
Decimation of her youth
War to end them all
Future widows will recall
Mankind mournfully only knows
War as history gravely shows
People may desire peace
But human nature is caprice

Michael J Pritchard

FROM NO-MAN'S-LAND

From no-man's-land, message from the wire
Gone are the fresh-faced young men, you once knew
Bravely they went down under fire.

From quiet shires to foreign fields
The great war would harvest all but a few
From no-man's-land, message from the wire.

Lost two regiments, happy new year
How their innocence would distort the view
Bravely they went down under fire.

The screaming whistle the rush of fear
And the forward ranks made death's rendezvous
From no-man's-land, message from the wire.

From foreign fields to quiet shires
We called so many and returned so few
Bravely they went down under fire.

Seeds of silence returned to the fields
While war-torn families prayed for news
From no-man's-land, message from the wire
Bravely they went down under fire.

Peter Herridge

SOLDIER BOY

'Over the top we go, lads'
He heard the sergeant's cry
Fear gripped his heart and held it tight
He didn't want to die!

The rain battered down
He was soaked to the bone
But better in the water-filled trench
Than where the bullets rang.

Boom! a shell exploded,
Closer than before
And he threw his hands
Over his head, sought shelter
On the trench floor.

Lying there amongst the mud
Tears stung his eyes.
He was only 21 years old
He didn't deserve to die.

He could see his girlfriend before him
How happy they would be.
Then he heard that voice again
It seemed right in his head
'Over the top we go, lads'
And the soldier boy was dead.

Roberta Holmes

WHITE LIGHT

He lay like some exotic desert bloom, open, red.
Just more knackered gear abandoned by the fools ahead,
All running from the fear of their fear showing,
While the watching hawk turns at the top of the sky.

Timeless layers of microscopic rocks. Unseen
Tonnes; unwashed, undirty. Windswept clean
And cauterized by aeons of unencumbered suns -
Pollution-free till his khaki flocks swept in!

He stirs and from his side a shadow creeps,
Like sap from a tree's untimely fell weeps.
Or sugar burnt: neither thin enough to seep beyond
The third level of carefully balanced grains.

It started like another humdrum PC game;
Same smug finger's devastating power. Same
Dumb targets - till a target fired back! The dark face
Wore a hatred not its own; moulded by a despot

On a shaky pedestal of power. When he killed
The boy the hatred slid away. Confused, mind filled
With all that crap that they were enemies, when just
A few wars back they said these were his friends!

So, no kindly morphine prick. No goodbyes,
Or greetings. Where now the light of God to guide
Him through the stalking night of crushing black?
The white tunnel people unafraid see

Before the final disappearing trick of death?
Equally as clever as the birth,
Yet only rarely are the tears those of joy.

The burnt sugar has set.
The flies have relaxed; the hawk is larger.

Alan W Ruffles

MY SOLDIER BOY

I live in the shadowlands
Without you at my side
No taste to my food
No meaning in my actions
Going through the motions
While my heart aches
With missing you
No joy in the long nights
The bed so empty
Without you
I yearn for the feel of your arms
Your words half whispered
In the dreaming time
I lie awake
Imagining the worst
Your body broken and bleeding
On desert sands
Longing for the moment
I step into the haven of your hug
Taste your lips with mine
I live in the shadowlands
Without you at my side

Helen Ambler

WAR IS SINFUL

Why do men hate each other? There seems no friendship anymore,
People get arguing and governments then start a war,
It seems so strange to me when people have everything they need,
They get so jealous of other people, then jealousy turns to greed,
If the world's wealth was shared with those who have none,
And people were happy and satisfied with the good deeds they have
done,
This world would be a better place, wars would then begin to cease,
Every country helping the other, this would be a place of peace,
We now have another war looming, there will be death and turmoil,
Just because a wealthy, greedy country wants someone else's oil,
Innocent people suffer and are killed for someone's greed,
Just because big nations want something they may never need,
Please Lord, let people live together in perfect peace and love,
With blessings poured down on Earth from your heaven above,
So that the sacrifice Jesus made when he died upon the cross,
Will be a worldwide victory and be the Devil's loss.

Stan Gilbert

TO A TERRORIST
(Matt 5 v44)

You are my brother, you are my sister,
I cannot hate you.
We share this Earth, its beauty and resources;
I cannot deny you space.
We both have weaknesses, we are not perfect,
I will defend your human rights.
If you cut me, I bleed; if you comfort me
Our bond of humanity is healed and strengthened.
Where is denial then? Where is hatred then?
Both are covered by compassion and love.
We are made in the image of God;
I must respect you and love you.

Joan Thompson

A WALL SO HIGH!

Two sides to hide
Behind a wall so high
Religious beliefs we take with pride

It all began long before my time
Whose war is it?
Theirs or mine

School is near for us to learn
The journey down our street
Is one we'll never earn

They promise peace and harmony
A wall so high the two sides paint
The same thing they want, peace and harmony

Karen Carlisle

POPPYLAND

(Inspired by the works of both Clement Scott & Thomas Cooper Gotch)

Barbed wire divides the fields
Churned ready for the seed
Any weed that settles
Is fed when the youth bleed
Shelling keeps you awake too long
Thoughts turn to distant Poppyland
Where stands a lonely tower
High above the sands

Cross the distant grey sea
Night's frozen desert sand
Beneath jungle storms of rain
Men lie in foreign land
She'll stand outside the cottage
As clouds colour in sunset
Crimson poppies in the field
And wonder why I'm not home yet

We'd wish a different harvest
Picking poppies from the corn
Sleep beneath a full moon
In the land where we're born
Don't wear them for the Generals
But for the lads in mud
The ones who gave their all
Paid in gore and blood

Cardinal Cox

1916

The guns and the streets are silent now, the butcher has slain us as
he would a cow, on a mattress in Bridget Moffets I lay, a burning lead
orphan in my gut he do play. Doctor O'Brian, his hands with my blood,
curses rebellion, for he feels that he must. His curses do sway me as I
drift through this dream, and sail ever onwards to old Skibereen.

As I lie here all bleeding, no reason ask why, for Doctor O'Brian, I see
in his eye, again curse the fenians of this bold gallant land, such stupid
young fools at Devalera's command. By my bed he do curse me and all
that I say, but his teardrops with my blood must mingle today.

On Bridget's cold mattress my life ebbs away, but sure it was brilliant,
for the fight fought today. So on this cold mattress made of barley and
hay, the post office in Dublin, freedom's flame it did blaze, for this
young man lies dying and O'Brian may curse, but sure I took no King's
oath or coins from his purse.

The room seems so hazy but my thoughts they still dwell, I can recite
all the speeches of Griffith and Parnell. I recall the greatness in my
veins it did flow, against a cold bitter empire we must overthrow.

So proud was I, a spirited young man, recited to Kearney of bad black
and tan, sculling pints in O'Leary's he agreed we should fight, if
written in speeches spoke truth of Erin's blight. Two sore heads in the
morning with new boots to be weaned, we marched off for Dublin from
old Skibereen.

We gazed and we wondered at Dublin's fine sights, Skibereen is the
place where fighting men fight, and then the next morning we made our
bold way, to fight shoulder to shoulder with the Dublin brigade.

I gaze to the window of Bridget's fine room, and out in the darkness,
a fine night she looms, far away from the gunfire and blistering shell,
'tis for Kearney, poor Kearney my heart tolls the bell, for how will I tell
them on his old mother's farm, was it not for my words, he would never
have borne arms.

Against a King and an army who have plundered worldwide, who have slain the best soldiers the world could provide.

The shells they were pinging around my young ears, the screams of the fallen for thousands of years, I found myself running from this mortal hell, 'twas then I found Kearney blown up by a shell. No final words beckoned from his poor blackened lips, I just held him and kissed him on his passage from this. If I could have been muted way back in my teens, then poor Kearney on his farm in old Skibereen could be tending the cattle, the sheep and the pigs, leave the well-dressed politicians to sort out all of this.

The dreams now all over, just too many tans, the betrayal and the prisons work according to plan, fine foolish words spoken, meaning only to jest, just bring to the slaughter the poor and obsessed, to man's blind indifference, for freedom we fight, from Bridget's cold mattress I must bid you goodnight.

Fergus Condron

WAR

Politicians are people who think they are right.
Through centuries of wars and demonstrations of might,
Millions have died and the suffering has been great
And the poorest of the people have had too much on their plate.
But how can we alter this unequal trend,
Let politicians and their cronies our homes defend?
Perhaps peace will prevail when their lives are at risk,
And the rest of us can get on with living in bliss.

A J Lawrence

FOR MY GREAT UNCLE ALAN
(The Conscientious Objector Remembered At last)

They wrote out in Geneva
a code to go to war,
but even after battle
a sniper knows no law.

I'd left behind the chapel,
though conscientious I,
and joined the Corps of Medics,
I thought, prepared to die.

For countrymen and king and land,
I went and risked my life,
I only left my mother
and sister, I'd no wife.

And they were sure that my white square
emblazoned with red cross,
would guarantee safe passage
and not another loss.

But war just isn't like that.
O reader, see the plight
of innocence or folly
in an enemy's gun-sight.

For Mr Churchill taught us,
though we never did it see
that man just never seems to learn
from war and history.

Tony Ball

IRAQ

Did you hear the injured screaming?
Did you see the red blood flow?
Did the roar of warplanes fill your ears
As bombs fell on those below?
Were you aware of families weeping
At the loss of daughter, son?
Did you feel no great compassion?
Was the battle really won?
It could have been your daughter
It could have been your son -
The innocents so cruelly maimed
Or murdered in the sun.

I wonder do you sleep at night
Or pray to God above
To give you strength to face each day
Proclaiming peace and love?
May God show his forgiveness
As we try to understand
Why we are used like puppets
In this brave, bewildered land.

Eileen M Pratt

STILL LIFE IN NEW YORK

The small Attic wine jug,
red on black terracotta
mid fifth century BC,
depicts the young man leaving
for that war in which the sons of Oedipus
contended for the throne of Thebes
and he would be killed.

Already armed with spear and shield,
his tunic neatly pleated, he receives
from his mother's outstretched hands
the plumed helmet
that was to cover his fashionable curls
for the last time.

In sunlight from a Fifth Avenue window
the intent figures
move still among the motes
perfectly describing a world's circle
to which no poetic line
is more than tangent.

John Weston

WAR

Cries of the innocent, worries of the mothers
High explosions, homes bombed
Soldiers dead, left to rot
Crackle of rifles, civilians dead
Many wounded by shrapnel
Blood left to decompose
Journalists fleeing, soldiers are captured
Many people reach a gruesome end
Counter-attack menacing, fighting continues
Soldiers called up to fight, times difficult
Civilians unaware of destiny, flee.

A buzzing of battling bees, handful of hissing fleas
Men on patrol, sickening sight of dead people
Odour of decomposed bodies, seclusion of mice
Firing ammunition, ricochet of bullets
Marsh of unwelcoming ditches, the silence of fatigued soldiers
Flutter of letters from home, herd of home lovers
Towering inferno of ghastly smoke, blanket of precipitation
Lives of soldiers endangered and turned upside down.

Ramandeep Kaur (15)

A FAUSTIAN RIDDLE

Man's spirit is forsworn:
a perverse contumely
lust shown
for war, a cryptic frenzy
in our time:
democracy dicing with lunacy?
Tanks and bombers a mime
for surplus oil, we see.

Looking at
the butt end of capital
aiming always to be fat
in a lawless carnival.
Shall man live by oil alone?
Faust's Utopian pitch
is a bad seed sown
by a wicked witch.

Faust, with cunning, you seek weapons
where none exist,
save those spawned by maverick cons
as crazily you persist
in this luxury of dreams.
Things nowhere to be found
have to be created by magic teams
of inspectors: a magician's ploy unsound.

The evidence? A tease
Faust cries out in desperation.
With customary ease
he'll bomb others into submission
one step ahead
or none at all
to re-enact an ancient city's fall.

Angus Richmond

ELEVEN FIFTEEN

It has been fifty years since then
When war was declared by Chamberlain
Hitler would not answer the charge
Of retreating from Poland, straight away
So at eleven-fifteen, on a Sunday
War was declared on Germany

The amount of destruction caused
Was so vast in its amount
That we'll never know the score
The death and the tears in their eyes
As we all said to someone our goodbyes
We will never fully realise

A rough estimate of civilians and soldiers
Who died is forty-five million
But there was total destruction
Of more than one nation

In World War II every country
Lost young and old men and women
They also lost their own children

Fifty years on we all remember
War, desolation that killed nearly every member
We all have forgot, yet remember
That all is not as it should be
We can't forget the people who died
Civilians, the Air Force, the Army, the Navy
But they passed away on both sides

Eleven-fifteen, fifty years on
There is no silence, the gun is still fired
Because people still caused war
And many thousands more will still die

Kieth T Jones

LEARN

Think of a man lying in mud and blood
Moments before, had before you stood
The why and the what-for was clear to them
The leaders had said they were the enemy not men

With honour and courage they obeyed and fell
Some survived and to us the horror did tell
Within the quagmire of death heroes were known
And through their example, mercy was oft shown

Soon this memory will be no more held in living mind
No witness alive, only the written word to remind
I say now was it madness from leaders sadly blind
Or was it just to relieve a financial bind

I did not live then, and more I must read
If there was a good reason, it wasn't hunger or need
But the honour of the fallen sowed a seed
There is a goodness in men and we should heed
Words written by those who in the front line bleed
And not allow any bad deed

Robert McGarry

TEN MINUTES

Only have a minute . . . maybe nine or ten
Just to say I love you lots, every day and when
We're body packed in trenches, though my thoughts are mine alone
To snatch upon those silly things . . . that make me smile of home

Only have a minute . . . maybe eight or nine
Just to say that I'm alright and everything is fine
I think today is Saturday though I'm not sure of the date
Only have a minute lass . . . maybe seven or eight

Only have a minute . . . maybe six or seven
Just to let you know my heart beats back with yours in Devon
I think about her green fields and the lanes we used to walk
You ought to hear the city boys . . . and all the things they talk

Only have a minute . . . maybe five or six
They've given us some powder love for all the lice and ticks
Thank God the kids don't need to shave, they wouldn't have a hope
With a sardine can of water just . . . and hard carbolic soap

Only have a minute . . . maybe four or five
Some men are humming on a hymn . . . I think 'With Me Abide'
The shelling's getting heavier now, much heavier than before
Only have a minute love . . . maybe three or four

Only have a minute . . . maybe two or three
The sergeant's telling us be brave all the lads and me
Once out of the trenches men give Jerry you know what
Come on boys fix your bayonets on . . . we'll show that ruddy lot

Only have a minute . . . maybe one or two
To write I got your letter girl to scribble I love you
And how are things with Mum and Dad, hope everyone's OK
Let them know I miss them all . . . each and every single day

Only have a minute . . . the order has come through
Remember what I've written lass, remember I love you
And on the day the baby's born, if I'm not there to see
Explain why Daddy won't be home . . . and hug our child for me

Only have a . . . .

M J Banasko

THE SOMME IN AUTUMN

A bright November sun
Clothes the hills with peace
Once the scene of hell.

Ploughs now gently till
The wide and fertile hills
Once ripped by blasting shell.

Burnished leaves now fall
And softly cover the scarred earth
Where once men fell.

Many autumns and harvests have passed
But ever these hills and fields
Of sacrifice and suffering will tell.

Helen M Seeley

SET IN STONE

The stone shines bright beneath the moon, beneath the twinkling stars,
The ground is marred by war and hate and torn by granite scars.
The memories fade in ancient minds unspoken by the breath,
The pages that the mind contains are buried in the death.
The soul burns bright in cold white stone, the rivalry never fades,
The stone holds stories that stay untold, trapped inside the grave.
Sights forgotten by those who saw, blind eyes trapped in the face,
The sightless death of those who fought, and died in this empty place
The stone shine bright, the moon rides high, the memory disappears,
The scars upon this ancient land show long forgotten fears.
So to the ancient, cold, black ground where hate and souls were met,
The memory is written in stone and mind. Lest we should forget.

Clare Hopkins

BOMBER PILOT

The night was lit by moonlight
With an occasional glimpse of the ground
Shell burst all around us and the engine's roaring sound
'Hamburg down below us,' Skip the navigator said.
'The target's down below us, keep going straight ahead.'
Two minutes straight and level in that time we could be dead
Then the searchlight hit us and held us in its grasp
Minutes to the target we made it there at last
Bombs away and upwards rose the plane.

The searchlights held onto us like glue
I swung to the left and then to the right
But that light held us in the night
Up came the flak thick and fast
Outer port engine hit, damaged by the blast
Fuel line fracture then came a glow
Shut it off and down we go
I dropped the nose and dived like hell,
I prayed we could pull out I could not tell
I would sooner crash than burn that's true
At last, I levelled a treetop height
The fire out we would make it all right
My heart in my mouth we started to climb and gain some height
Now left behind like a pregnant duck
To get us back we need some luck

The compass out, the navigator dead
The course all to pot, the Channel ahead
'If you ever prayed boys now's the time
I can't gain height, I cannot climb
Fuel now low, may have to ditch, boys down we go.'
I pulled up hard and on the stick in one desperate plan
'O Lord above we don't want to die, please give a chance,
One more try.'

Very slowly, very slowly up she goes,
Our spirits now high with the runway in view
Will have a bed tonight and not in the blue

The runway lights just switch on,
Wheels down, safely run
Another op over, may tomorrow come slow
For come the night up again we go.

Gate Keeper

CIVILIAN RESPONSE TO THE SINKING OF HMS SHEFFIELD 4.5.82

Such a sad face
staring back at me from the mirror.
Why so sad?
You've brushed your teeth,
combed your hair,
put your slides away over there.
There's a bright moon and
dazzling stars to gaze at through the window!
Why so sad a face?

Ah yes . . .
. . . Those faceless men aboard a ship
so very far away.
So many men who'll never see another day.
A missile exploding;
Hearts thumping,
Fire, pain and
Cold, cold sea on all sides.
Screams of dying men,
wounded, fighting the waves,
crying for rescue.
Bodies received unto the deep.
There are fatherless sons
and wives who weep.

So I've combed my hair
and brushed my teeth,
and I'll go to bed -
- But I shan't sleep.

Katie Norton

DAWN, NOVEMBER 11TH 1918

I awake once more to the sound of rain,
The floor of our trench is awash again.
Six inches of water, six inches of mud,
A black stream of urine, vomit and blood.

The roar of our guns, shells streak overhead,
I lie on the fire step, wishing the enemy dead.
The word's gone around, at dawn we attack,
I look at my friends, will any come back?

I think of my brother, also serving somewhere,
And pray he's still breathing God's good air.
My thoughts fly to home, my wife, Mam and Dad,
From me they'll not hear, that things are so bad.

The green clouds of death have come and gone,
Leaving only those able to get their masks on.
The sound of a sad song floats along the trench,
The voice carries far through the clamour and stench.

The sweet smell of death hangs over the ground,
Across no-man's-land rows of wire surround
A hundred deep shell holes filled with mud and water
And mules and men who died in the slaughter.

Many rumours abound, a truce will be signed,
Soon war and its troubles left far behind . . .
Dear God, the sun has risen, soon our guns will stop,
The captain blows his whistle, together comrades, over the top.

Brian J Toomey

WAR AND PEACE

War is a tabloid and a mirage which could paralyse the stronghold of a nation's tenacity and lead her to unpeaceful situations which build up indestructible walls of insecurity, violence, depression, anguish, suicide and mass murder. War is the maker of destruction while confusion is the first born son of war. While peace is that protagonistic figure seeking the welfare of unity of the totality of the human race, whose glory is the harmony of understanding.

The walls that put up the struggles and imbalances of the middle east seemed translated with a piloting flame and it created the craving of the mindset of setting the flame. *The black smarthy* (Niger Delta of Nigeria) stood, standing voice high above the catapulted wave of fear waiting for the wagging of the horror visitor. Then, in within them a voice was heard, the voice of warhood, the grenades had splintered, the town was racked by violent conflict while there was a spiritual vacuum of war that was filled with violence, high incidence of depression, anguish, suicide and mass murder, they became swarthy and scorched the war's imprisonment.

In the banquet hung the banner wheeling the voice of war. Still amidst these, the social revolution pushed forward, blaring in the glowing light of peace and the only panacea that lit the eyes of everyone was the word peace but that solace was wrapped in the mantle of confusion. But the unfulfilled dream of a peaceful ecological atmosphere never died as they were still seeking peace as never before.

Those who left war-torn areas became refugees in their own country as peace had hung in the cleft and covert refusing to be seen or to be caught in the rugged mountains. Like the new dawn, like the fair moon, like the bright sun, the fragrant powder of hopefulness smoked in the cliffs with none to behold him. Man worked for peace, he walked towards it but its acquisition is his enemy because he knew not the way. Who is the prince of peace?

Awusi Endurance

UNTITLED

Can you feel the insufferable sulphur rush
Bubbling amongst your blood?
No pain is felt, no odour smelt,
Yet a red-black thick as mud.

Little ladybird, do you feel no guilt
Sticking in my throat like glue?
A lump of sin with burning eyes,
Searching for the taste of Jew.

A world of sulphurous hearts and lungs,
A race chewing Hitler gum,
It's free for all, God's dishing it out,
There's plenty for everyone.

Katy Fulker

HUMANITY

We were given this earth,
For us to live upon,
But it doesn't seem long,
Until all will be gone,

Man has the theory,
That one should rule all,
Destroying each other,
Till all will fall,

Let's live in peace,
And share this gift,
Stop all the war,
It's time to shift,

So all can enjoy,
The award of life,
Without any pain,
Or any great strife.

Alan Gordon

COMMANDO MEMORIAL

The wind-song from the surrounding hills,
Mingles with the heartfelt sigh of emotion.
As Commando veterans stand before this memorial.
The very clouds that lord over this valley,
Dip as they sweep past in admiration.

The winds carry on their declining perturbations.
The sounds of men in vigorous training tasks,
A mountain crag to conquer, a stream to ford.
Forced marches at a pace to take the breath away,
The skirl of pipes as a bridgehead seized.

The wind-song never to be muted by time.
Nor the deeds of valour forgotten.
Nor the names of comrades fallen in the field.
This happy band of hero-warriors.
This elite of ancient Britain's arms.

Strong emotions of pride and accomplishment,
And sadness too. The price of freedom secured,
From a ruthless, yet courageous enemy.
They stand before this replica of flesh and blood.
Each with memories coursing through their souls.

How fitting this location, a land of heroes bold.
How appropriate the wind-song's deep lament.
As though a host of kilted pipers resurrected.
Fill the air with reverent sounds of former glory.
It takes a hero to know another in this art of war.

Alistair E Brown

NO ONE EXCUSED

Hubble bubble reduced to rubble
War-torn, frightened in a huddle
Panic induced from lack of news
Rumours reign and turn the screws
Hearts attacked by shock of shelling
Memories racked, no fortune worth telling
Through crescent and star the holy smoke curls
A final pail of silence hurled.

East and west in burst of bubble
Razor'd sharp in search of stubble
Tightened noose in lurch to bruise
Spark is loose in search of fuse
Leaders descend and sense their power
Advisors recommend to issue the hour
Hot line frantic, a deadline to send
A failed deterrent, is this how it will end?

Trigger is pulled to no turning back
Signpost signed and the mirror crack'd
Mushroom is opened to gale force white-hot
Dust ever falling, the sky it will blot
Buildings lie twisted nothing worth saved
People have melted, no need for the grave
No taker of prisoners SS20s and Cruise
No point, no use, no one excused!

Keith Robbins

TO ALL THOSE

To all those in fields of war,
Blue skies of battle, conflict out at sea,
Praying for peace, fighting for liberty.
To all those with spirits of fire,
Nerves of steel, hearts of oak,
Whose eyes were blind from gas and smoke.

To all those who gazed towards the horizon,
Never knowing they would never look back
And those whose sweethearts wed in white,
Only soon to be dressed in black.
To those with photographs next to hearts
With courage and with will,
Face to face in mud, no choice but to kill.

To those who lie beneath the earth
Who watched blood spill and tears flow
And friends, comrades, brothers in arms
Left dying in the afterglow.
To all those we remember
And may we not forget,
Because the time may come
When it's too late for regret.

Andrew Handsaker

UNTITLED

Like a bat out of hell he came,
In his Heinkel aeroplane,
Chuck saw him just in time,
In his Spitfire he climbed,
Turning his Spitfire he descended again,
Opening fire as he came,
The Heinkel turned and rolled away.
But back it came with great speed,
His guns a-blazing, to do his deadly deed.

Chuck soared up again and came down low,
The Heinkel took the full force of his blow,
Turning and spinning out of control.
Down to the ground, Chuck saw it explode.
Chuck wiped the sweat from his brow,
He'd come through but he didn't know how.

With not much fuel and a damaged plane,
He limped back over the Channel,
To Blighty again.
Arriving at his base safe and sound,
Chuck was pleased to be back on the ground.

Chuck was shaking as he left his plane,
He knew how close to death he came,
He gave thanks to the Lord,
For bringing him safely home
For he knew only too well,
Come tomorrow where he would be
Fighting up in the sky again,
To keep England free.

Mary Wills

WAR, 1916

'Over the top, boys, over the top!'
The guns and the mud, the stench and the thud
Of the shells - I want it to stop!
'Over the top, boys, over the top!'
I trudge in the sludge of the trench, feel a nudge
And he whispers, 'The enemy's near,
Can't you feel his hot breath, see the Angel of Death?'
But we have to keep on in the dark or the dawn
Though we're shaking with fear.

Thick clinging mud and the ominous thud
Of the shells;
A sickening stench of death in the trench
And the yells!
I feel my legs sag - 'What's that in the bag?'
Is the CO's demand,
'Rubbish, Sir, if you please,' - I sink to my knees,
I can no longer stand,
For I know the truth - it is all of the youth
We could find!

The roar of the guns, the shouts of the Huns
I could stand,
But dying like that! - worse than a rat -
Wasn't planned!
He was only a boy, an innocent boy,
But he copped it today,
The dark, endless mud ran red with his blood
When they took him away;
Now I trudge on alone in the sludge with a groan,
And I pray.

Betty McIlroy

REMEMBRANCE DAY

Standing proud, standing tall
Awaiting the fire of the cannonball
Two minutes silence is all it takes
To remember those who died for our sakes.
They died for peace, though we have it not
War still goes on, but they're not forgot.

They volunteered to fight the fight
And kept their enemies in their sight.
Today war veterans of all kinds
Search memories that linger in their minds.
Standing proud to remember those they lost
Who fought the wars at any cost.

Remembrance Day will still live on
For our future wars have not yet gone.
Death will happen and that we fear
But today we remember those most dear.

Nicola Joy Moore

BEN

*(In memory of my paternal grandfather who fought
and was seriously injured by shrapnel in the first World War)*

I remember my grandfather in his wheelchair,
Huddled in pain, although there was no despair.
He recalled; 'I've raised three sons and had a good life,
Tho' I couldn't have done it without my devoted wife.'

He smiled weakly, 'I fought in the Great War you know,
Oh yes my dear, it was a lifetime ago.
I went away as a fit young man
And came home battered and broken as only war can.

Our training was short, our losses were great,
Replacements were needed at an unprecedented rate.
In the heat of the battle on foreign land,
I heard the squeal of a mortar as I fell to the sand.

An angel drifted towards me when I woke,
My vision was a field nurse who gently spoke;
'Your war is over, it's Blighty for you son,
Most of your battalion is lost but the battle was won.'

I still have a deep gaping hole in my side,
I think of those I fought with and remember with pride.
I am on my way to the great reunion on high,
No tears dear, for now, it is my turn to die.'

Theresa M Carrier

A SERVICE OF TWO MASTERS

From Scotland we came
In the year of our Lord 1863
Civil War raged in the Americas
Whilst I served two warriors, Grant and Lee

Men torn apart by victory and shells
As a Virginia lass stole my heart
So far away from home and highland
A sniper by method and design

Stamping out men's dreams
Within an eye-blink
An instant in their time and life was gone
Feeling nothing, being nothing

   Other than
Executioner, premeditated instructions
Formed by the Devil's desire.

James Patrick Milton

REMOVING BARRIERS

Many hours spent in preparation, conflict resolution,
even just for a few hours' conclusion.
No one job done, by any single person,
as each must cover - every eventuality.
Counsellor, advisor, driver, friend and leader,
correlator, initiator - reality prohibited.

Time flies with a consuming fashion,
pick up points changing to drop offs.
After a few hours - devoured like passion,
but still the staff, have more to do.

Evaluation, de-briefing, problem sorting,
then unwind from the stress of reporting.
Some socialising and bonding,
but naturally this time - nature responding.

Most of the work - unseen and unknown,
by any person who's never held the post.
Father, brother, sister, mother and leader,
all responsible - yet always responding.

Receiving insurmountable and inhumane insults,
for removing myths and stereotyped barriers.
But using integrity and ability of unity,
keep going on bonding - interdenominationally.

Through cross community work and insurrections,
creating harmony and interaction of youth.
With community relations - pushed by faith,
as only removal of inherent fences will win - truth.

Progression with slow and steady resolve,
creating programmes with a professionality pace.
Gained only through time and experience,
removing barriers with a constructive grace.

Gary J Finlay

WHY?

why are flags upon the lamp posts
and paintings on the walls
signifying bigotry and hatred
they are christians after all

will politicians, ever find a compromise
between the shankill and the falls
will they listen and take notice
or heed the people's calls?

the winter nights are here again
still gunmen on the prowl
they plan the deeds, their hatred feeds
with faces twisted in a scowl

because of their religion
someone innocent will die
the victim, will never sense the danger
nor have the time to cry

be it a catholic or a protestant
- the outcome's still the same
another murder victim
and another night of shame

somewhere, a child will ask its mother
why has daddy not come home?
will he be coming back for christmas
why does he never phone?

god put us here upon this earth
to know and love each other
not to murder kill and mutilate
and use religion as a cover

the rewards for living such a life
as the gunmen will discover
for them, the path to heaven will be blocked
they will have to take another

they'll have a warm reception
and forever they will dwell
with lucifer their lord and master
in the eternal flames of hell!

T Britton

A SHIA DREAMS
(This is a poem about a Shia leader
(Ayatollah Mohammed Bagir al-Hakim)
who was assassinated
in Najaf, Iraq, using a car bomb)

In awe of May
And reluctant prophets.
I call on Ali . . .
Crawl into the mind of God.

63 years . . .
Ring any bells?
A Shia dreams
As children capture the aroma
Of betrayed petals
And the stench
Of another lonely suicide.

A desert fire . . .
Extinguish me ocean.
Joviality burnt out . . .

Rain for Najaf?

John Hobbs

A STRANGE WARTIME MEMORY

Four tall strangers during the war
Boarded the morning train,
Long, dusty, brown robes they wore
And their faces showed signs of strain.
Round their waists were bands of string
And round their wrists and ankles too.
They didn't carry a single thing
Yet they'd journeyed from afar I knew.
They didn't sit on the empty seats
But stood silently side by side.
Were their robes stuffed with things
That they were trying to hide?
A whistle blew, and then the train
Entered a tunnel as dark as night.
Then I saw brilliant flashes of light
Sparkling and shining, a dazzling sight.
Rings set with diamonds without a flaw
That seemed as large as the Koh-i-noor
Were worn on the fingers of these men,
The like of which I'd never see again.
Here were treasures of unknown wealth,
Carried by foreigners of stealth.
Did they bring funds to help the war
Hidden in the dusty robes they wore?

Margaret Nixon

SOLDIERS

Look, the children,
listen, don't guess
behind their eyes.

Sing God, unsmiling.

Scar, bone, flesh.

In the dark
small figures shake,
shiver, cough, cry out.

Daylight, trek.

Glenna Welsh

TOMMY AND YOUNG 'UN

'Can you see me Tommy?'
Said young 'un.
'I cannot see your face
I know you are near brother
I can feel your breathing
In this dark and lonely place.

Can you hear me Tommy?'
Said young 'un.
'I have run my last race
I'm glad you are near
Good old elder brother
This alone I could not face.

Can you hold me Tommy?'
Said young 'un.
'I can go on no more
Did I serve my country?
Will our mother be proud?
What is the point of war?'

Tommy held his brother,
'Goodbye young 'un.'
Wiped the tears from his eye
Still now the breathing.
At peace amid the chaos.

Seventeen is too young to die.

Anthony Warwick

CHURCH AND STATE

Men in top hat and those in mitre
telling it is time to live
and time to die.

A time for prayer;
a time to fight
and a time for them to lie.

It has ever been thus.
People called to rescue church and state
with sacrifice of young men's lives.

Would that men in top hat and those in mitre
be first in muddy trench.
Among bloody bodies they sent to die.

Robert Allen

DS DAY

April 19th 2003 VB Day
Victory in Baghdad
December 14th 2003 DS Day
Defeat of Saddam

Hiding in a hidey-hole
To the south of Tikrit
Found by American soldiers
That bearded little . . . demon.

Hope the same thing happens
To another bearded beast
Named Osama bin Laden
For a peaceful middle east.

H G Griffiths

WHERE BUTTERFLIES FLY

Children die,
Where the butterflies fly,
Where the song birds sing,
Comes the weapon with sting.

Fired by malicious man,
From his cruel harsh hand,
To the screaming cry,
As the children die,
Across the meadows or desert,
To the city street,
Buildings collapse,
Exploding head to feet,
Murdered,
Under the name of war,
Little children,
Will laugh no more.
Parents left hysterical,
Devastated, heartbroken,
No more to their babes,
Will words be spoken.
Gone, gone, gone,
By some manic man's,
Official callous command,
Childhood stolen,
In a missile's flash of death,
Children slump,
With no more breath.

Children die,
From the unleashed violent,
Brutalised by moronic man,
Children become silent.

Leaders pretend to be humble,
Apologies tumble,
Who is hoodwinked?
For justification leaders fumble.

'Sorry, it happens sometimes,' leaders say.
'Civilians and the innocent, get in the way.'

Children die,
Where the butterflies fly,
Where the song birds sing,
Comes the weapon with sting.

Children die,
And you and I,
So shocked, are left to cry.

Carol Ann Darling

THE ATTACK

Sun shining
Birds singing
Wind sighing
Poppies swaying
Men dying
Wounded crying . . .

Green shoots waiting khaki clad,
Peaceful fields where languid cattle grazed,
Now stained red with martyr's blood . . .

Shells exploding
Earth erupting
Machine guns rattling
Grenades sounding -
Slaughter heralding infamous day . . .

Madness reigning
Horrors defying
Death surrounding.

Arthur Pickles

ALI ISMAEEL ABBAS

His name will live on in our memories. This little boy with poignant
looks has lost his whole world to western greed.

His parents and other members of his family are dead. He lies in a bare
hospital bed with no arms, little hope.

Shameless people in his own country fight, steal and desecrate,
even going to the extremes of robbing hospitals.

We were told there were weapons of mass destruction in Iraq.
Ali and thousands like him have suffered because of this.

The worst weapons of mass destruction are used by the Allies.
They are dropped continually on innocent Iraqi people.

Shoot first, ask questions later! How can you ask questions
when your victims lie bleeding in the dust?

We are told the soldiers are heroes. How heroic can you be
when you have all those vastly superior weapons?

Where has civilization gone? Have we come so far that we can *still*
make war on Ali and other defenceless people?

What next? Who next? You, me? The more we kill and maim
the more likely it is that we'll be destroyed too.

The coalition war cabinets are the real terrorists in this world.
They have the technology to wipe out vast tracts of land.

What horrors will this war bring down on our heads?
There *will* be reprisals. More innocent civilians will suffer and die.

They will die because of the greed of their leaders.
Any thinking person knows this war is about oil, not Saddam.

Allah please bless little Ali Abbas and all the other Iraqi children,
animals and people whose lives have been torn apart in the name of
avarice.

Daphne Richards

NEW ENEMIES

How can those who kill and maim
Be never overcome with shame
How reconcile their vilest deeds
When many grieve and many bleed?
The tears are real of those who feel
The loss of dear ones, in coffins sealed.

How can they face a world which sees
Their works of horror on TVs?
Works which twist the world askew
As *'greater'* terrors they pursue
While those who blessèd peace implored
Have their heartfelt cries ignored.

By whose name and for what cause
Can they deny these sacred laws -
The right to life and liberty
So lightly held by you and me?
Some call on God, their cause to be
Blind to such outrageous blasphemy.

Brian Ford-Powell

I DON'T WANT/I WANT

I don't want to be sad,
Anymore.
I want to be happy,
That's for sure.

I don't want to cry,
Anymore.
I want to smile,
That's for sure.

I don't want any wars,
Anymore.
I want peace on Earth,
That's for sure.

I don't want to fight,
Anymore.
I want it to end,
That's for sure.

I don't want revenge,
Anymore.
I want your love,
That's for sure.

I don't want sorrow or pain,
Anymore.
I want truth and harmony,
That's for sure.

S Longford

SOLDIER BOY

Look out there, you soldier boy.
It's no-man's-land, so feast your eye
Upon the desolation there.
But don't stay long to stand and stare.
You might just get your head blown off,
And never more you'll live to quaff
A glass of wine, a pint of ale,
Or feel the rain as cold as hail.
This is the cursed Western Front,
And we are here to bear the brunt
Of what the enemy throws our way
And pray we live another day . . .

Let me tell you, soldier boy -
It is no joke, you've got to employ
In a grinding, crushing, war machine.
In fact, the worst there's ever been.
The chance you'll live is very slim.
The outcome will be very grim.
The noise, the flying shot and shell
Will make you think that you're in Hell.
Don't stop to dream upon the way -
Down in a shallow foxhole stay.
So mark my words, you soldier boy,
In war's cruel games, you're just a toy.

Joyce Haigh

THE VOLUNTEER

I've been submitted to the battle of the gore
Now I've joined the First World War
A landscape of craters, wire and mud
Am I to be valued for the good?
Will I fight in the greatest battle
Or will I succumb to the machine gun's rattle?
Will the bullets pass me by
Or will they kiss for me tomorrow's goodbye?
It is the morning of the day, the big
Guns fire - I'm over the top -
Through the wire - through the
Rattle of the machine guns' fire.
We've secured the enemy's trench
And all about me the dead, and oh!
Oh! The terrible stench. I'm alive.
I've survived another day of fire -
Tomorrow again through the wire
The cacophony of death rings through
My ears - and yet tomorrow no more tears -
I'm oblivious to it all.

T McFarlane

OLD SOLDIER

There are long
heat wave days
when nothing happens.

An old man
with pale eyes
in a crumbling head
sits stiffly silent
on a wooden bench
at a wooden table
in the woods;
picnicless,
expressionless;
a blank page.

An old soldier
barely alive -
just sitting.

Gwil Williams

FOUND IN A FIELD

The pilot's body,
Identified by metal tag,
Fell from afar
Into the soft earth and
Rotted to a bag
Of bones. Now we wonder
Who's lain in his stead
For fifty years.
It's here the man's been found,
Remains exhumed
By the indifferent plough.
Was his coffin filled
With sand and stones?
People need to grieve,
Mourn heroic death
Then look for life to come
And believe.

Nancy Rudden

A VALIANT SOLDIER

This poem is a tribute
To the uncle I never knew
For he was called to the colours
To serve in World War Two

Called up to oppose tyranny
From the land of the rising sun
And the heel of the Nazi jackboot
When I was only one

He was but one of many
Sent to the far east to fight
To help the Burmese people
Repel the Japanese might

It was in the Burma jungle
One fateful rainy day
That a deadly Japanese sniper
Came across his prey

Hit by the sniper's bullet
That he never ever saw
And his live was over
Another casualty of war

He gave his life for king and country
And for the likes of me
So that I may live my life
In a country that is forever free.

D W Mynott

I SCREAMED IN SILENCE

The poor with chattering teeth, silent,
With frozen hands and feet, staring
At human greed, the innocent,
Adrift, unheard are left starving.

I screamed in silence at the world,
And beat my chest, tears fell like rain,
My sanity remained, though I stumbled,
Not alone, others felt the pain.

The mother's mind now lost, insane,
Abandoning her child to fear,
The tears of father's cheeks do stain,
For children taken, wars do sear.

The world's horrors not hidden now,
Displayed in graphic detail, why,
Do children watch and cry or know,
I screamed in silence at the sky.

Beauty imprisoned, lost to hate,
The lives so precious, what is wrong,
Are thrown on fires of Hell, to fate,
Do you not hear the reaper's song?

No hate, no war, no famine, no tears,
Our journey short, we understood,
A peaceful time for future years,
I screamed in silence at my god.

David M Walford

FALLEN HERO

Huddled like a foetus
He sits cradled,
Rocking his body
Backwards and forwards
In an epileptic motion;
His bloodied hands hold
His face, to hide him from
This insanity;
His ears are witness to the
Screaming shells that fall
And eternally scar.
The cries of death and its
Stench fill the air,
His band of brothers, no more.

This hell on earth distorts him,
Disfiguring his boyish seventeen,
An afflicted twist of fate
For he is at war now, and not
At the game;
His punishment is, to follow his father
To love his land, his home,
To fight like a soldier
To die like a man,
When in truth he's just a boy.

Susan Marie Andrews

THE FRONT LINE

Upon the front, the torment reigns
There's no tomorrow of heavenly gains
A second blast. A shot or call
I turn around and see them fall

No one can pretend. It's real
I hear a shell, some shrapnel, feel
I watch dear Pete, his leg blown off
And rip my jacket made of cloth

A siren overhead of me
I wonder does this mean I'm free?
I know I'll live until tomorrow
Despite the stench and heartened sorrow

And as I dream of coming home
Reflections clear. I'm so alone
Please God give me some last hope
And give me strength enough to cope

Then as dawn creeps another day
Blood shed conjures on its way
I jump in deep myself to drench
And shelter there within this trench

Bullets firing overhead
I duck then see my mate fall, dead
This crazy madness. Please help me
Live for today. Don't take from thee.

Vanessa Jane Haynes

WHAT PRICE WAR?

So this was war.
They stepped forward, the intrepid ones,
Eager for action and adventure
And those who doubted, hid it well
They had no choice
'Go forth and make the future brighter.'

And this was war
With deadly bombs and treachery,
Made bearable by selfless comradeship.
With flying bullets and no place to hide
A moment's pause, a gleam of hope, and then
Once more, inexorable, inexplicable.

A woman screams,
A child runs out, uncomprehending, 'Come back!'
One scream amongst so many, silenced suddenly.
Stand tall, desolate child, don't cry.
Your tears will not placate the guns
Nor clinging arms, nor pleas, waken the dead
For this is war, your future will be brighter,
It was said.

June I Holmes

REMEMBRANCE

On Armistice Day throughout the land
All ages gather in the cold to stand
In silent respect and give a salute
To the war dead who were resolute.
Ghosts of the past are resurrected
Memories of comrades recollected
Moments recalled of self-sacrifice
By the valiant who paid the price.
Comradeship and esprit-de-corps
Helped to face the pain of war
Of endless hardship and great sorrow
Endured with hope of a better tomorrow.
Now with hindsight we question why
So many people had to die
But on reflection there was no choice
If freedom was to have a voice
To oppose the unjust tyranny
Of terrible crimes against humanity.
Death comes to us all eventually
But sadly in war prematurely
Many lives lost with bodies dismembered
Grateful survivors ensure they're remembered,
Their sacrifice and loss has been our gain
And those who died didn't die in vain.

Bill Newham

TWELVE RED ROSES

The guns are silent and the Great War is over
No flowers on the field, not even some clover
Devastation and misery are present, everywhere
And John lay dead, his youthful body laid bare

This was the war to end all wars, so they said
But John is now asleep, no pillow for his head
His battalion was pinned down with enemy fire
And his Captain lay injured beyond the safety wire

He had to be saved or otherwise he would die
John said he would get him, or have a good try
The trenches were a maze, going this way and that
So John crawled to where the Captain was at

Guns were firing and bombs exploding all around
Soldiers kept their heads down, almost to the ground
But in their hearts they felt John hadn't a chance
The distance was so great and all they got was a glance

The guns stopped firing and there was an eerie still
Then a screeching noise was heard, like a turning mill
Some distance away, John was pushing a barrow our way
And inside was our injured Captain, unconscious and grey

John collapsed with blood oozing from an incision
He died there and then, having completed his mission
He was later awarded the VC for being so brave
And now each year, twelve red roses decorate his grave

William A Laws

Iraq, November 2003

It is a long fought strife that we must face
To win the minds and souls throughout Iraq.
Religion, custom, habit of a race
That we have conquered; yet somehow we lack
Some understanding of their way of life,
When never they have know democracy.
For always they have lived beneath the knife
A despot wields, to force his policy.
How can they understand, when we march in
As foreigners, and 'infidels' to boot,
And tell them we have come only to win
Their freedom, liberty, and not to loot
Their country of its wealth, but just to give
Its citizens the right in peace to live?

Christopher Head

THE BATTLE OF BRITAIN

Goering's murder squadrons packed in tight formation,
came to smash a way, ready for invasion.
In Messerschmitts and Heinkels came the Luftwaffe's might,
the RAF were waiting and ready for the fight.

They served us well, those men in 'blue'
a gallant band, but oh, so few.
Yet odds were nothing to compare,
to what those men fought in the air.

They searched the sky for the crooked cross,
and showed those Nazis, who was 'Boss'!
some grimly smiled - some cracked a joke,
as each Luftwaffe plane went down in smoke.

Their watchword was, 'They shall not pass!'
Kings of the air - they were first class.
Heroes all - those mighty *Few,*
remember those men and give thanks too.

They patrolled the skies from dawn to dark,
their bite was much worse than their bark.
And each vapour trail up in the sky
would see another Nazi, 'passing by'.

They flew the air on wings of speed,
the deadly Spitfire was their steed.
And in Hurricanes of equal might,
they put the Luftwaffe planes to flight.

Near three long months they fought and died,
they knew no fear - they never shied.
God gave those men that dauntless power,
The Battle of Britain was their finest hour!

G F Davison
(The Poetical Gunner)

2003

Death has honed his scythe
Readying to glean war's dead.
Death's dug deep in bloodied earth
Dug deep to cover
Bodies and entrails.
Nature's kin, to rot, corrupt
Staining earth's shell with indelible finality.
Death spreads his cloak, dark sky skimming
Harbinging endings, not beginnings.
The last, final passage,
Unwatched, unprayed for or laid out;
A solitary happening.
Death's unleashed the horses
Thrown open limbo's doors
Blood painted Hell's portals.
Death has prepared
Death has planned
Death's cooked a feast
Of lust, famine, betrayal, fire.
Death invites all to partake.
Thrown wide his arms,
Turning, whispering; 'Follow me,
For I am invincible, war's hero
The one and only victorious,
For I can never lose.'
Death has honed his scythe
And once the call has brayed
Will lead, lead on
Twisting and gathering to destruction.
For death has honed his scythe
And misery will walk beside.

G J Pledger

LOOKING FOR PEACE

I am dead they say
A soldier of many wars.
Yet I walk the battlefields
Looking for comrades who also
Are dead, they say.

From the mud of Flanders and
The blinding sands of the desert
The stinking jungles with its
Pungent smells of death.

I keep looking for a lasting peace;
Must I walk for ever to find a resting place?
Keep marching solider
On, on . . . for ever on!

David G Bromage

TANKA

Standing near a tree
Whence all the leaves have fallen
It appears to me
Like a ship without a sail
Ready to withstand a gale.

Standing near a tree
Which has lost its golden leaves
Tall against the sky
Like a sturdy mast or pole
To meet winter's snowy role.

Mavis Downey

THE ANNIVERSARY

A veil of mourning cast
Because of the Great War
The Armistice anniversary
Memories still raw

Silent queues of mourners
Pile the Cenotaph with flowers
Soon to be as dead
As the numberless in Flanders

Lists of fallen inscribed
On monuments to those who died
Town and village count the cost
Of every single son they'd lost

Hopefully, time will heal
With every year that follows
And poppies will grow again
Upon the fields of Flanders.

Ann Donovan

MY GRANDAD WAS A SOLDIER

In 1916 my grandad was a soldier
Fighting in the mud of the trenches
Amongst the blood, death and stench
Caught up in the 'war to end all wars'
He never got over the horror he saw
Talk of war and his fists would clench
Perspiration his body would drench
When reliving the chaos and slaughter
Hearing the explosions and screams
He survived but his mind was unstable
At night the noise pervaded his dreams
To escape he drowned in flagons of ale
Unhappy and coming apart at the seams
Remembering each battle in vivid detail.

Rosemary Davies

THE POPPY FIELDS OF FLANDERS

The fields are bright with poppies red,
Looking so proud as they sway their heads.
Remember Flanders and the young men who died,
We will never forget them our hearts fill with pride.

When the poppies are blooming, like a tribute to the brave,
They are all in God's kingdom, not there in the grave.
At night when we dream of the fields of red,
Our loved ones are remembered as we lay in our bed.

Like the seeds of the poppies scattered far and wide,
Men and boys fighting side by side.
Look at the poppy fields with peace and love,
One for each soldier in our home far above.

One day when the world lives in harmony,
No more wars, mankind living free.
From the highest mountains to the desert sands,
We will walk through the poppy fields hand in hand.

Esther Annette Davies

THE PRICE OF FREEDOM

A long time ago
There were boys left home
To journey afar
And face the unknown
Went off to war
With high spirits; good cheer
Resembling a party atmosphere
But it wasn't 'over by Christmas'
And the war dragged on
Conditions were atrocious
There was nowhere left to run
Some came back with injuries
Some were maimed for life
Most lived with the memories
Of the suffering and strife
But so many never made it home
And died in foreign lands
The war graves and memorials
Testaments that stand
To all those mother's son's who went -
Fathers, brothers, uncles too -
Went and laid their lives down
To give freedom to me and you
They didn't ask to die so young
They didn't ask to be heroes then
But that's why we wear our poppies
So we don't forget any of them.

Dino Carlin

REMEMBRANCE!

In foreign fields in lands afar
So many brave men died,
They died so we might live
To follow the Righteous Star!

As we must remember,
That special day in November,
We must never forget
The ultimate price they paid!

So let us look to the skies
With resolution in our eyes,
As we watch the petals fall
And remember, they gave their all!

W E Clements

FORGIVING LOVE

He stands in the dock,
Found guilt of the crime,
Too late,
For him to turn back the clock.

Wave away,
An appeal for mercy,
No more any one, on his behalf,
Can say.

He's a heartbroken parent's son,
Parent's anxious cries,
Of heartbroken feelings,
Asking why, in their eyes.

An ordeal they wish they could alter,
His parent's forgiving love.
A bridge over distressed waters,
A bridge of forgiving love.

Poppy Fields

REMEMBER

All the men saying goodbye,
The women trying not to cry,
Kissing the children while they are sleeping,
Can't stand to see them weeping.
Down the street to catch a train,
Will they be coming home again.

Not so long ago, they were boys,
Playing with their favourite toys,
A car, or maybe a train,
Will they be coming home again.

Think of how they must have felt as they walked away,
And don't remember them for just one day,
Think of all the suffering and pain,
And those that didn't come home again,

Two minutes isn't much after all,
Think about it and it makes you feel quite small.
Silent prayers we say and in our hearts they remain,
God bless those that didn't come home again.

Maureen Arnold

TO SOME SOLDIER

Sleep peaceful, contented sleep, brave
long-dead soldier. 'Neath verdant lawn,
or brambled hedge may be thy grave.
For Memory watches constant as the dawn,
that one day, years long past,
bathed the blood-stained field
where you did breathe your last
pained sigh, and felt your spirit yield.

England thinks not once a year
but every day of thee. The gift
you gave was all you had. Fear
departed when you thought, 'Lift
on high Freedom's flag'. Never
would you laugh, love or know again
Peace, that fruit of your endeavour,
for Death your opening life did drain.

We did not see (being too young)
your youthful faces or hear your laughter,
still, when'er we find ourselves among
soldier's graves, we hope that now and after
this brief life, our land shall ever thank
you in those silent trenches lain,
and know that you who fell and sank
in War, did not live and die in vain.

Anthony J Brady

REMEMBER ALWAYS

Fighting and killing, man against man
Has been going on since this world began
But do we remember the family or friend
Who died in the hope that all conflicts would end.

They went into battle, gave up their lives
Fighting for freedom, for husbands and wives
All left behind whilst they went to war
To be slaughtered in millions on some foreign shore.

Power over others has been the main cause
Of so many conflicts, battles and wars
But there is only one with control over all
And He is the one on whom we should call.

We must remember with reverence and love
Our comrades now resting with God up above
Whilst we offer prayers that all wars will cease
So that we may all live in comfort and peace.

Bill Brittain

UNTITLED

In our churches for them we pray
I feel sorry for the ones that's left
The mothers and the wives
When the Sheffield got sunk that day
Their loved ones gave their lives
RIP.

H G Booley

BULLOUGH'S WALL

It was sixteen a side football against Bullough's Wall,
With the lamp post a corner and the old gate the goal.
The kerb was a full back, there was no offsides.
Barb wires topped the bar, the pitch two streets wide.
Size ten clogs wove a delicate trace
With an old rubber ball or case without lace.
There were no referees, it was free for all
As England beat Scotland along Bullough's Wall.

Along came the summer, long days from school.
It was fifteen a side cricket against Bullough's Wall.
The wickets were chalk on the loading bay door,
The gutter the crease and the post box a four.
Over the cut it was six and out
And the next one in was the loudest shout.
There were no LBW's, no bails to fall
As England beat Australia, along Bullough's Wall.

And some played at Wembley in a cup final dream
And some played for England on Lord's velvet green
But some fell at Ypres and some on the Somme.
And some fell at Delville on the way home.
And those that remain pay out their toll
With satanic toil inside Bullough's Wall.

Hayes Turner

FIGHTING FOR PEACE

Something of an oxymoron, the peace-fight.
Yet sometimes we must fight to win the peace.
Belligerents provoke, threaten our right
to live as we would wish, without surcease.
So out comes all the spin, the jingo-lingo:
our spurs can jingle-jangle with the best.
The war becomes another game of bingo,
our men mere members at warlords' behest.
What irks beneath the gross indignity:
what lurks beneath the shadows of deceit:
our involuntary zest for gross malignity,
rewaking those primeval lusts we beat.
The greatest danger we must meet head-on:
believing all the spin that we are fed on.

A century and a half has come and gone
since that Death Valley charge sent men to glory
in the Crimea. Lessons learnt were none
as witness this brave world's re-echoed story.
Though every conflict throws up men of worth
whose sacrifice is sculpted that restores
some faith in human nature, hope for Earth,
the boast's naive: the war to end all wars.
Like lower animals out in the wild
we act, react, in ways our reason cries;
the war-whoops hide the truth: the keening child
whose threnodies and dirges dull the skies.
We'll wear our poppies, grateful, sad and proud;
acclaim our heroes' prowess - not too loud.

Adrian Brett

RELUCTANT HERO

He never wanted to be a soldier,
Didn't dream he would go to war,
He imagined he'd be like his father,
Sail the seas, see the lands he saw.

He never wanted to be a hero,
Didn't dream he would kill those men,
He imagined a foreign foe,
'Shoot to kill' merely words till then.

He never wanted the shame or glory,
Didn't dream he could feel so cold,
He imagined the media story,
Then shoot himself, eighteen years old.

Betty Lightfoot

MUD

The men with red eyes wade through the liquid mud,
Heading for the angry guns coughing up bullets again.
Wishing they were back on the duck boards, before
The screaming bullets take them down with a heavy thud.

As they march on through the shell holes full of red blood,
Their thoughts go back to their youth, the only escape from
This hell on earth, trying to find some corners of sanity;
A place to run and hide away from the engulfing mud.

It won't be long before their bodies can rest and melt away,
They will soon be dreaming of a distant place in another world.
They have played their part out well and taken the falls like heroes,
Their words will drift away like the wind, they will not see the next day.

The next line will come just like the last; to start again the ongoing
conveyor belt, to take the place from the ghosts drifting away,
above the fields of sunken eyes. Waiting to move into the fear and loss
from what's just gone before, to get ready for their own departure,
and leave behind their cards that were dealt.

Ricky N Lock

LA BANDERA (THE FLAG)
(Somewhere in Mexico, 1912)

In a village to the east of the mountain
Miguel Arconada was laid to rest,
Father Alfonso conducted the mass,
and prayed for Miguel to be blessed.
Miguel was a soldier,
and upon the casket the flag of the nation was laid,
And prayers were said for his untimely death,
for the ultimate sacrifice paid.
There were tears from his mother,
his sister, his brother, oh, how they cried,
They cursed the men who lived by the gun,
they were the reason Miguel had died!

In a village to the west of the mountain
Ramon Torrado was laid to rest,
Father Roberto conducted the mass,
and prayed for Ramon to be blessed.
Ramon was a soldier,
and upon the casket the flag of the nation was laid,
And prayers were said for his untimely death,
for the ultimate sacrifice paid.
There were tears from his mother,
his sister, his brother, oh, how they cried,
They cursed the men who lived by the gun,
they were the reason Ramon had died!

Like a forest fire for ten long years
the hell of the revolution raged,
Death and destruction walked hand in hand,
as though the devil had been uncaged.
And all the people who fought in that war,
they all believed their cause was right,
So many funerals were held in many villages
for those who'd perished in the fight.
And upon the caskets were laid the flag
of the nation for which they'd died,
Red, white and green, on caskets all over the land,
same flag . . . different side!

Juan Pablo Jalisco

THE SADNESS OF REMEMBRANCE DAY

I remember with sadness the Remembrance Day parade
Remembering battles fought when other countries invade
The Queen and Prince Philip laid their wreaths of red
Prince Charles, the Duke of Kent, paid their respects to the dead
Princess Anne, the Prime Minister and leading Politicians
One laid for the Queen Mother who has seen many repartitions

Then two minutes silence and hush all around
The last post, then a military band broke the sound
Then the march by began, with the lower ranks
Those of the Military and Old Soldiers who drove tanks
The Nurses, the Land Army, the Boys' Brigade and the Scouts
And children watching and wondering what it's all about

There were Pensioners who fought in the First World War
And those who were rescued from the Dunkirk shore
The Airmen who fought their war in the sky
Never ever questioning or asking why
Those in the WVS, Ambulance Crews and Firemen
Who dealt with the bombing in such hard times back then

White helmets of Russian Convoy Men stood out in the crowd
Comrades of my dad, I felt sadness and yet proud
The Evacuees and the ARP men who patrolled the streets
And the Bevin Boys, working down the coal pits so deep
Two of them lived with Grandma and with fondness she would say
'The boys taught you to walk while spending hours at play'

At the end of the parade the Queen Mother wiped a tear
As she remembers the bombing, the terror and the fear
Young and old together, their respects were paid
But the memories of war must never fade
Lest we forget those who died and the ones left behind
For they died for freedom and the good of mankind.

Celia Law

AND THE POPPIES FELL

Soldiers, sailors, airmen,
Solemn faces in this hall did dwell.
Singing hymns of praise to God,
And the poppies fell.

The trumpeter played a fanfare,
Sad thoughts in hearts did dwell;
Then two minutes silence came
And the poppies fell.

Fluttering down 'midst man and boy,
Each had a tale to tell.
Young and old in harmony,
And the poppies fell.

The lone trumpeter sounded the last post,
Brought tears no one could quell.
Tear-clouded eyes filled with memories,
And the poppies fell.

Dorothy Kemp

REMEMBRANCE
(Dedicated to Tom Weedon)

The light shone through the window, the dust danced in its rays
I sucked a fluffy Polo, flicked through my 'Songs of Praise'.
I can't remember shopping yet I hardly have to try
To recall my shock that morning when I saw my father cry.
To me his brother Horace was just another name
A badly tinted photograph fading in a frame.
That morning saw the ending of my childhood in a way
Brought home to me the heartache and the sadness of this day.
All those soldiers killed in battle each and every treasured one
Had once been someone's brother, someone's husband, someone's son.

Marguerite Holloway

SANDS OF TIME

Frozen in the desert sand
Laughter echoes not a sound
Smiles and frowns on each one's face
The look, an end of human grace
Where they stood is where they'll stay
There in time to decay
Silence, disaster, faces of fear
Their graves forever silent, in the sands of time.

Caroline Halliday

POPPY DAY

Unreal these poppies
that we wear like badges.

Better they should bloom in fields,
bright, transient, fragile,
as real poppies are.

Better again, a wand should wave
and we should see churned fields
of torn-limbed soldiers;
remember sundered vows of:
'War no more!'

Blobs of blood are poppies.
Unreal these poppies that we wear.

Jacqueline Ives

REMEMBRANCE DAY

Today is a day set aside, for us to remember?
To remember all those that have given all there is to give.
We know and believe, that they are waiting to be with us,
At the end of this our life's journey, we remember them.

They made the journey so that we can live in a better world
There were other times when each day they gave their all
So that we others may lead a life, or be given the chance to.
We remember them, they are many, for whom we set aside one day.

To remember, those that fought in wars for the good of others
We know that they will never be forgotten
They are gathered together now, as we recall them, name by name
To all those that lost someone we send our love to ease their pain.

I walked in a field of corn and there was one poppy
I remembered them
I walked in a field of poppies and there was one head of corn
I remembered them
That I can walk this world as I do I shall never forget you.
I remember.

It is with sadness, that I feel for all those that were left behind.
It is with joy, that I know that they believe, we will meet in time
That we can walk with hope, and peace in our earthly ways
We thank you, you who have suffered, to give us these days
You, the ones that will gather with us at the closing of life's span
With your memories and love for those that have given all they can

We remember them.

Ian T Howard

MATTY

On Remembrance Sunday I stand with pride,
I hold a small cross with a poppy by my side.
I'm here to pay tribute to an uncle of mine -
No time to know him, I was a child at the time.
I stand with other people who feel like me,
We think of all those fallen heroes, whoever they may be.
The minute silence stills the air -
We want those no longer here to know we care.
I stand and reflect, my thoughts go deep -
Of death, destruction and the endless sleep.
What were their thoughts as they faced their foe?
Were they afraid? I would like to know.
The enemy you faced was human too,
The bullet is fired - for one of you, life is through.
Could you hear the screams above the din?
Did you think of your family, your kith and kin?
I sent you a photograph, which you carried with you,
After all those years, the message I wrote is still clear and true.
All those young lives gone from the face of the Earth,
I pray people will always remember what you were worth.
You are all lying in graves in far flung places
But God above knows each of your dear faces.
Although I was young, I recall the heartache your family bore -
Losing you Matty, made so many hearts sore.
So each November I think of you, Matty, with great pride.
A son, a brother, an uncle and the life you were cruelly denied.
Wars still go on, no lessons have been learned -
Peace, tolerance and forgiveness have to be earned.
I pray for a world where wars will cease,
Then, God willing, we will all live in peace.

Elizabeth Hoggett

2003: THE FALLEN OF IRAQ

In the year 2003, warmongering insanity reigns
In Iraq, remember the dead and what remains,
What have the US and UK been doing there?
There is only so much bloodshed we can bear.
What is the real purpose of this armed invasion?
With such little convincing honest persuasion,
A tyrant of Tikrit removed, US chaos remained,
Innocents are still being shot, killed and maimed,
Weapons of mass destruction was the reason,
For this cruel and dishonest, murderous season.
These weapons would have hurt us, they said,
An ill-conceived invasion, so many heroes dead.
Guantanamo Bay detainees - their rights abused,
Our loved ones over there we pointlessly lose.
One country cannot truly dominate another,
To successfully subjugate a sister or brother,
Our armed forces defend our land with sense
And are *not* political weapons of governments.
No lies or 'spin' can hide what is clearly true,
As our politicians try to mislead me and you.
Our troops are dead and dying there, for a lie,
No WMD found, no matter how hard they try.
Iraqis say we are just no longer wanted there,
When our heroes are killed, they do not care.
Suicide bombers sacrifice themselves, incredibly,
This madness for something they will never see.
Wars are supposed to stop an evil or an injustice,
Why do terrorists hate the free world like this?
Remember the fallen of Iraq, no reason to die,
These heroes are dead, and we do not know why.

Christopher Higgins

RATTLER

Don't show any fear
She could see you so clear
From so far away
And now you're too near

She's guarding her den
And you've overstepped
Your heart recoils in mid-beat
Of the Diamondback death

That rattles your throat
As you try not to choke
On the venomous dread
Sliding down your backbone

In the heat of the sun
A sudden chill in your nerves
Frozen over in stone

As her buzzing alarm
Reverberates in your soul

You try to stay calm
It's all in the stance
But the panic is rising
In your shaking hands

And then
            she strikes - fast!
And it's just too late
To try to escape
The razor sharp
Grip of fate

And you awake
     in the dark
From a cold sweating prayer
Knowing how close you'd come
To not being here.

Steve Gunning

SEVENTEEN IS TOO YOUNG TO DIE

Down in the Flanders mud he lay,
Arms thrown out in a grotesque way,
Unseeing eyes staring up at the sky,
Seventeen is too young to die.

Back home in England, asleep in her bed,
The young soldier's mother unaware that he's dead.
When I tell her the news, she screams and she cries,
She wants me to tell her it's not true, it's all lies.

I have the courage to tell her it's true,
For that young soldier was my son too.
War is the ultimate ugly lie,
Seventeen is too young to die!

Anthony C Givnan

FLANDERS FIELDS

Young men standing in a row
Waiting for the word to go
Marching feet all in time
Along this silent, frightened line.
Soon the whistle could be heard
Silent troops don't say a word
Louder whistling getting nearer
Inside these men the actions now clearer.
Now load your rifles and take your aim
Your life will never be the same
For bodies litter around the floor
Those young dead men will march no more.
And as the dusk of battle falls
The rifles will be heard no more
The dead are now all laid to rest
Each one of them had done their best.
So on the fields all these years later
The poppies slowly sway
They show us where the soldiers died
And where their bodies lay.

Linda Francis

CLICHÉS OF THE WAR

Weapons of mass destruction
Secretly in production
Despite the solution
Offered by UN resolution

Rules of engagement
Are causing enragement
To coalition forces
Cavalry with tanks (not horses)

Psy-ops is the tops
When winning hearts and minds
Smart weapons, do on average
Cut down collateral damage

Progress of American forces
Peace protesters' angry voices
Liberation by invasion
Eviction by the coalition

Following the Geneva Convention
The Americans are, without reprehension
Excepting that, they
Omit to mention Guantanamo Bay

The Republican Guard dug in and waiting
The push on Baghdad, their war not abating
Hope against hope to inspire
Yet another case of friendly fire

The Brits are holding their key points
Await to deploy their ordinance
But only when the generals decide
Which Iraqi is on whose side

Lines of supply
War birds in the sky
The plans have been laid
For emergency aid

George Bush, Saddam Hussein
Tony Blair, the runaway train
The die has been cast
Who knows how long this will last?

But us spectators have a 24 hour call
On TV, radio, papers and all
And we get to see and hear every minute
Of every bloody thing that's in it!

Reuben D Faro

FIGHT THE GOOD FIGHT

'In Flanders Fields the poppies blow . . .'
A plea for peace if ever one was heard?
Sadly no, not so, for carefully mark,
'Take up our quarrel with the foe . . . ,'
Thus hate survived so many needless deaths,
Were last breaths used to curse? Yes, clearly so:
Had hundreds of thousands died in vain
In blood-soaked mud and pouring rain?
Go on fighting, do not yield,
That more may lie in Flanders Fields.
Ill-led, ill-fed young men had paid the price
To make a fairer world, but were denied;
So many lessons were left unlearned,
But one above all remained intact,
Always go on fighting, do not yield,
As long as there are more for Flanders Fields,
Each year the poppies will bloom in vain,
If you, or I, or others must fight again.

Bill Fletcher

WAR WITHOUT REASON

Here we are on the field of conflict once more,
Someone has found reason again for us to go to war,
It's politicians saying that WMDs are the cause this time round,
Makes a change from munitions kings wanting to make a few pound.

They used to cry out when they badly needed employment,
Sending men to their deaths seemed to be a source of enjoyment,
Now though, it's other financiers who are seeking their fame,
Not the man in the street, he is only a pawn in this game.

Roll up! Roll up! It's all the fun of the fair,
Or that is the attitude of this man, Tony Blair,
I can't see him getting killed in the rush,
He won't be at the front, nor his mate, George W Bush.

When they start to lead from the front then I might make a comeback,
I am bloody near eighty but ready to don my back pack,
Then we'll see if they are cowards meeting the enemy at a pace,
With our bayonets up their backsides, they won't dare to 'about face'.

One of our greatest leaders, Winston, he knew how to lead,
Men fighting in his day were a different breed,
In the first world war, he was in the First Sea Lord's seat,
In the second he was at the front even in Downing Street.

On occasions he would venture out to see how his lads were doing,
Not sitting at home billing and cooing,
You have a long way to go - Bush and Blair in cahoots,
Before you are both capable of filling his boots.

But then again if Winston had been here to deal with this lot,
He would have left it to the UN to come up with a plot,
After all he was one of the founder members after World War II,
He trusted them in future cases as this - knowing what to do.

Jack Edwards

IRAQ WAR: THE AFTERMATH

Suppression, after all these years
has ended in a brutal war;
sweet liberation now, not fears
delights Iraqis, rich and poor.

But victory caused a statesmen frown
when civic discipline broke down.
Unprecedented! Soldiers watched
Iraqis, used to being quashed,
rise up in fury with one aim -
to show their hatred of Hussein
by looting palaces and homes
and shouting, 'Freedom!' from the domes
of Baghdad's mosques and city squares -
with none to censure he who dares!

'When the lid blows off the kettle
the oppressed will show their mettle.
It's happening now. Let us agree
Iraqis want to prove they're free!
It's right for them to rage and jeer
at years of subjugated fear.'

Fine words from Bush and Blair, who learn
first with horror, then deep concern,
of libraries burned, old folks attacked,
hospitals robbed, art galleries sacked,
the prisons open, killers flee,
two hundred mentally ill set free;
the aged tumble to the floor,
their stolen beds dragged through the door;
vigilante groups are formed
to stop civilians' homes being stormed.

There is no order, chaos rules;
is this what liberation fuels?
The coalition, unprepared
for urban fury it had bared,
had not the men to bring control -
and soldiers say it's not their role
to arrest looters, lend a hand
to stop them raping their own land.

This is the mayhem wars create,
'til rage and greed at last abate
and leaders, taking law in hand,
bring order to a savaged land.

Leigh Eduardo

JIHAD ESQUIRE

when i was killed in the third crusade
    my heart ejaculated joy
i could join the saints and martyrs
      being righteous, though a boy
         being right was preordained
         being right was soon attained
being right brought pain and death
    being right's a wicked ploy

David Xeno

TWO LETTERS FROM THE SOMME,
BOTH ARRIVED 18TH JULY 1916

Dear Mrs Beck, I'm sorry, but your son was killed today.

Dear Mam, arrived here at the front, just where I cannot say.
I'm not allowed to tell you, but don't worry I'm alright.

Be sure he died a hero's death. He fought a valiant fight.
We were crossing over no-man's-land, the guns were close and loud
When he fell. He didn't suffer. You must be very proud.

I know you told me not to lie, but I look an older fellow.
I had to come out with my pals, they'd think that I was yellow.

I didn't know he was so young. His acts belied his age.
I feel honoured to have known him. Yours sincerely, Captain Page.

You know how much I miss you, Mam. I'll live by what you said.
I know you've always loved me, so forgive me. Your son, Fred X.

Ann Wood

IN SERVICE TO A KING AND QUEEN

*(Dedicated to all national servicemen who served, be it in war or peace.
Particularly to our young brothers-in-arms who served in the Palestine,
Malaya, Korea, Cyprus, Kenya and Aden emergencies 1947-1962. With
special remembrance for those whose young lives were lost during
National Service and for whom final demobilisation never came.)*

1939-1945
'Long live the King'
Loud rang the loyal cry,
All for 'King and Country',
When the war loomed nigh.

From far and near
Soon came they all,
From colony and dominion far,
Answering well this country's call.

No matter were they young or old
Or long, or short, or tall,
On land and sea, and in the air,
All fought as warriors bold.

Long years of war and battle fought,
And won brave victories,
To right the wrongs that others brought,
By land, by air, and o'er the seas.

At long, long last, came peace to all,
And to loved ones did then return,
Returned they home to country proud,
The long, the short, and the tall.

1947-1962
'Long live the Queen'
Though peace and calm did reign,
The young men of the country
Were called to arms again.

North and south, east and west,
Went out the rallying call,
Jock and Taff, Mick and Brit,
Were enlisted, one and all.

To diverse camps, in many zones
Were sent to learn the rules,
On how to fight in modern times,
Well learnt in many schools.

Their trades and skills did benefit
All ranks and manners of men,
Though on demob from service,
Were never used again.

For 18 months, or 2 years hence,
When time was not their own,
No matter then what ere the gain,
Were happiest when going home.

Edward James Williams
A Bystander Poet

ANOTHER WAR

Another war started by fools.
Another war built on a lie.
Another war in which children will die.
Another war that won't be over by Christmas,
Another war in which a journalist,
From his hotel window
Can tell us that
Missiles landing in the city
'Lit up the sky like the 4th of July.'

Ah well, that's all right then.

R A Westlake

TEACH OUR CHILDREN NOT TO FORGET

I bow my head in silence, each Remembrance Day,
And think of how each hero, sadly passed away.
I think of how each hero, died upon strange lands,
Then lay beneath the sun or moon, with rifle in their hands.
I think of folk who sailed, sadly lost at sea,
And wonder if at last, they're now just sailing free.
I think of those who flew, each mission they would dread,
And as they got towards their goal, what thoughts were in each head.
I never flew, I never sailed, I never marched to war,
I never had to watch, my friends die by the shore.
I never understood why soldiers had to fight,
And when I asked, my father said, 'It's just wrong from right.'
So each Remembrance Day, when my head's bowed real low,
I close my eyes and visualise the places they would go.
I think of how each hero, for others had to die,
And that is when I bow some more, and for each one I cry.
Remembrance Day we honour, we mark it with a flower,
To show that we have not forgot, each hero's finest hour.
For if we don't remember all the lost that be,
We all too soon may honour, the dead of World War Three.

Sid 'de' Knees

IEPER

England was the dahlia garden, where to toil and reap
and where to romp and rest,
England was the heirloom mattress,
where would meet the tide of birthlings with her breast,
England was the buffet oaken bartop,
crescent-cloyed and speckled blonde,
By a million pillioned porter pots,
seared, come tepid, tamed and cold,
Forever gone,

Ieper was too shy in torrid anguish
from the tremoring and bickering and farts,
Ieper was the kissed and frozen killer in the muzzle,
It was nothing in the heart;
Save unwant of remnant stewflesh,
sent to fortify - to spur the lion on,
Yet it soon dedaubed the trench head,
Seared, come tepid, tamed and cold,
Forever gone.

Tom Hathaway   _

A FALSE ADVENTURE

As I sit here at the fire-side
staring vacantly at its flame
I think about the Hitler war
and how I joined this brutal game.

I had only reached my seventeenth year
but I lied about my age
I thought enlisting would be an adventure
until I got to the adult stage.

But my idea of adventure
in my years as an enlisted man
was not what I expected
so it did not work to plan.

We were shifted round the country
to where army billets were erected
there we were trained in the use of arms
until our skills were then perfected.

Then we were shipped across the sea
to Africa's burning sands
where we managed many victories
and chased the Germans from these lands.

But with all the bloody battles
my adventurous spirit died
when I saw the deaths of comrades
and began to question the reason why.

Lachlan Taylor

UNTITLED

He tilted his head, straightened his back
Remembered the sound of the rifles' crack

Beads of sweat, streaming into his eyes
Listening to the mournful cries
He'd done his best, was not enough?
Now court martial plays it rough.
Coward they called him there on parade
So many friends had died in that raid
Mercy he pleaded, none to be given
Back to the hole once more he was driven.
He thought of that night, first impact
Tried whistling a tune, Britannia in fact
Mouth was so dry, lit up a fag
War was becoming a mighty big drag.

When first he enlisted he felt he was big
Just sixteen, never learned how to dig
They gave him a spade. 'Get shovelling Son'
This was the moment it had begun.
His best mate Fred had been the first
He saw the wound where the bullet had burst
This wasn't what the poster had said
'Your country needs you' his young brain was fed.
He had slipped away to mutter some prayers
The 'shakes' had taken him so unaware
Now of course hate from his friends
Warned him too, his life would end.

After all these years we've learned a lot
We know this man a coward not
They give it a name, too damn late
A pardon? Maybe, at St Peter's gate.

Soralen

TOMORROW NO SORROW

I watched your heart, so full of sorrow,
For you would not see me tomorrow.
I watched you place a single rose,
With thoughtful tears, for where it goes.
I saw you dry away, many sad tears,
At thought of spending the lonely years,
I know that life, may appear, surely bleak,
But I wish that you, could hear me speak.
For life goes on, and you must know,
That time heals all, and surely so,
And I can no longer call out your name,
Nor hold you close, and comfort your pain.
Although I am here, right by your side,
And surely have my arms, held open wide,
For I was not ready, but I had to leave,
And all I can do now, is watch you grieve.
I will ask that God, will hold your hand,
And that with time, that you will understand,
For one day, you will be here, next to me,
And seeing this too, just as I now see.
Please do not grieve, to wish me there,
But simply 'cause you miss me, love me and care,
For life with its never ending, sure, steady pace,
Must make room for another, to take my place.

C R Slater

A PROMISE MADE . . . A PROMISE KEPT
LEAST WE FORGET

I saw the rows of stone, white graves
In Florence, Italy
And my promise made so long ago
Had now come true for me
My feelings! Well, I can't describe,
The right words I cannot convey
But, with whispered breath I said, 'I'm here!'
Upon that bright October day.
The name upon that soldier's grave
I read with tears and pride,
And as I lay my flowers down
I thought of *why he died'*
My brave young uncle gave his life
For freedom's blessed name
And when I gazed at all the other graves
I knew more young men had done the same.
All so young had sacrificed
Their lives for you and me
Had fought and died so far away
So that we could all walk free . . .
So, here at last in Florence
As I stood and read his name with pride
I whispered. 'I love you Uncle Jack,'
And I just wish you had not died!'
And then I wept my proudest tears
For my *promise made* had now come true
And as I kissed that blood red rose
I said . . . 'I'm here at last *to honour you.'*

851805 Bombardier J F James Royal Artillery
6th April 1945, Age 25 Ubique Quo Fas Et Gloria Ducunt
Not just today but every day, in silence, we remember
wife Molly, Mum and Dad.

Written with much love and pride and dedicated to my Uncle Jack, (John Francis James) who gave his life for freedom and peace in Florence, Italy in World War II at the age of 25 . . . and who's war grave I at long last visited in October 2003 along with my daughter Nicola and granddaughter Aneliese. The first members of the family ever to do so in fifty-eight years . . . I'm proud to say . . . I finally kept my promise to you Nanny . . .

Also in loving memory of my beloved mum, Ethel May Murphy who never lived to see me keep my promise, but who I know was there beside me on that October day in 2003.

Sylvia E L Reynolds

GRANDDAD

Granddad had a bald patch, down the centre of his head,
Plastic teeth instead of real ones, that comes out when it's time for bed,
He was not a perfect specimen, with stubble on his chin,
Hairs in his ears and up his nose, I still would not swap him.

His skin was wrinkly like a prune, shoulders slightly stooped,
After Sunday dinner, on the sofa he laid, full up - bloated - pooped!
He would tell me all about the war, and the small part that he played,
Then he produced a small-carved box, with ivory and pearl inlaid.

As he opened it he told me, not to let anyone ever know,
About his precious medal, that to me he was to show,
It was brownish with a ribbon, *For Valour* engraved around the rim,
He had to go to London, where the king handed it to him.

As Granddad got much older, for long periods in his bed he would lie,
Mum and Dad said I should prepare myself,
                                        for Granddad was soon to die.
Granddad's now gone from this world of ours, as a friend a terrible loss,
However his love for me continues, for he willed me his Victoria Cross.

Terry Sorby

ULSTER

While the blood of the innocent still runs through,
Then Ulster, I will always cry for you!
How all the mothers wish for a new and different day -
That will finally come and wash all our blood and shame away!
All those countless killings for their own just cause.
Children grow up, never knowing whom their real father was
And so on! This old hatred will spread
From the kindred old to the ever increasing new.
Always subtle in their passing, such a contagion
And truly poisonous view.

Here we all stand, in this truly futile war.
While our holy politicians, outwardly condemn the killings.
Yet secretly they scream for more!
How can I be proud?
Yet, I want to hide my very face,
From this phoenix-like war -
In the damned, home place.

Victor Shaw

REMEMBRANCE DAY, 11TH NOVEMBER

Wars are not started according to God's will - only the Devil's strategy!
In trying to maim, kill and destroy all the good lives God has given.
So we'll not only think about them on Remembrance Day -
But until we all meet in Heaven.
Dear Lord, keep each lost soul safe, knowing their ultimate sacrifice
Has been given.
Also, shelter in Your love, all their loved-ones left behind
And dry each and every tear.
Exactly how they would have wanted and done so
If they were now here.
Now let us all salute with pride -
All servicemen and women, this present time
And honour those who sacrificed their all -
For mine and thine.

M Ross

REMEMBRANCE SUNDAY

It was on Remembrance Sunday
That I sat on a seat in the park
From a nearby church I heard singing
Of hymns, and the sound of a lark

The canons and guns have retreated
The soldiers of war have grown old
With God's grace and love of one's neighbour
Only stories of war will be told

But in far away countries, there's fighting
With deadlier weapons than then
We pray for these demented creatures
That we hardly think of as men

Agonising cries of the innocent
Explosion of bombs everywhere
Bloodshed and killings of children
The Peace Plan ends in despair.

Audrey Petersen

REMEMBRANCE DAY

Memories, memories, memories
of a time, long ago
now over half a century - be it so!

10,000 parading on this Memorial Day
Marching, silently marching, a sea of faces sway,
marching alongside feet that make no sound today.
Remembering those who died in conflict -
on this special day not forgetting those at home,
who worked and waited there.
And the courage of countless citizens, bombed
almost everywhere.

Greater love has no man, that lay down his life
for his friends.

So sad, so very sad, alongside the limbless,
the blind and the deaf.
The old veterans, with their brightly polished medals
proudly marching by, shoulders back,
their heads held high.
Trying to hide their limps and pains,
as they look up to the sky.
Some, for the moment, still think they are in command
and shout the order to salute the Cenotaph, as they pass along.

Tears roll down my face and each year the more I cry
as I watch the dear old faces of these men and women march by.
Who once, were very young, bravely going to war, eager to fight
for their country and fearlessly face the unknown,
and like so many (my love was one) never to return!

Now nearly 60 years on, I only see how old they look
and it makes me feel so sad and I wonder how many
will be marching next time round, as their time is running out!
After they are gone, who will remember them?
No doubt they will go down in history in the next millennium!

As I shed my tears and think of those long war years
some of which were very happy and some so sad,
with many tears.
Then suddenly I realise, I must be a veteran too
for when the war was over I was not quite twenty-two.
I sometimes wonder what my love would have been like,
if he had lived to this day - which forever stays in mind.
The verse we hear mostly on this Remembrance Day . . .

They shall not grow old as we grow old,
Age will not weary them or years condemn.
At the going down of the sun and in the morning
we will remember them.

When I hear the last post I still shiver to this day
for those who were loved and lost -
long gone away.

Edna Parrington

REMEMBRANCE SUNDAY

Each dying year when the Armistice Parade
Snaps a smart 'eyes-right!' to the stiff-stood Mayor.
I note the dwindling members who assemble there
Behind the willing bugles of the Boys' Brigades.

And I remember her who secretly shed tears
When that foul obscenity, the First World War
Silenced a well-loved voice for evermore
Right at the end of those four, fateful years.

Her unrequited love was multiplied
By later generations who went away
To be maimed and mutilated and who died
In untold thousands, every day.

That is why when that day comes again, early each November,
It is they who waited 'till they could wait no more
that I remember.

Dan Pugh

*(The lady in verse two was my foster mum in the 1930s
and the well-loved voice was that of her elder son.)*

PMs Wife

The man I married ain't no war Merchant,
But I'd blow him up if he said it was urgent.
'If you draw up a proposal, I'll get down on both knees -
Guide your mass weapon into me.'

'Darling PM, I've got a raging election!
Pass the law, then pass some protection.'
Behind closed doors - 8b/10 -
Bedroom politics defied by men.

Expensive cabinet at our party for two
'Champagne for me, brie for you . . .
Hold a referendum when you're unsure,
My love for you is Parliament pure.'

Dave Percival

ASLEEP

Tread softly, as we lie asleep
On foreign soil but do not weep.
We, who never will grow old,
Who once were brave, upright and bold.

Young we were, our future bright,
And shone before us, in our sight.
Now we band of brothers, lie
Together, near God's cloudy sky.

November breezes swirl and blow
The poppy petals to and fro.
Silent and white, the marble stones
Lined like soldiers, over our bones.
But we will stay, as ever thought,
For freedom wins, our lives were bought.

Gwyneth Pritchard

WHITE MARBLE, GREEN GRASS

Count them now while all is still,
Stark white crosses, massed in ranks.
Sentinels to mark some passing,
All within green grassy banks.

This is no normal field of death,
Where families tend and children weep
But far away in some distant land
Where foreigners, doth tend and keep.

Why are they here instead of at home?
What did they do that was so wrong?
That they should be left here where they fell
Not forgotten but alone for so long.

So Tommy and George and all you others

We'll count you now, while all is still
Bright, white crosses, massed in ranks.
Proud sentinels to mark your passing.
Where you lie between green grassy banks.

John Osland

EAGLE'S WING

Soldiers' true . . .
Of the red, white and blue.
We thank God
for each one of you.
War happened early in Spring . . .
taking flight on Eagle's Wing.

Carol Olson

WAR

Our lives are very precious
Upon this fragile earth,
War should be discouraged
Encourage all new birth.
What do they gain in fighting -
Killing all in sight
War is such an ugly word
Does the slaughter make it right?
Does it really have to be?
Families killed on both sides
Showing no one mercy
As thousands fall and die
The war cries are for freedom
Does it make us free?
I think we all should gather,
Take our lives very seriously.
For if we go on fighting
The human race will fall,
No one can live in harmony
If we build upon this wall.
To be the sole ruler
Over all mankind.
Don't let it be, think right now
It's not too late, you'll find.

J Naylor

WHEN

When will there be peace,
When the world has no war?
When will people live in harmony,
When the people starve no more?

When will we feel safe,
When the streets we walk are pure?
When will we stop dying,
When the sick have found a cure?

When will our nations unite,
When the world has no hate?
When will colour have no meaning,
When the people alter our state?

When will we share true love,
When the people have no fear?
When will we love all people,
When the people share each tear?

When will the people stop taking,
When the people start giving?
When will they want to share,
When people care for all that's living?

Rose Murdoch

SELF-DETERMINATION

Shadows marched along the wall
Where angry men would fight and fall
Bullets cut through dialogue
Amidst a plot of crimson fog

Battle cries, alone were heard
The hunt for truth but too absurd
With every soldier there to fight
To put an enemy to flight

Oilfields beckoned 'Help us! Come!
Rescue each and every drum!'
America and Britain came
To seize it all, their common aim

Invasion forces guard it all
Ignore the mass Iraqi call
For self-determination now
This freedom that they won't allow.

Kim Montia

Watching For A Sailor

Please do not keep waiting for me
Nor keep a watch out to the sea
I know the pain and ache inside
And many tears mixed with pride

The day I set out from the shore
We vowed our love for evermore
How could we know what was to be
That my return you would not see

But my love, your life is young
You must not wait where I belong
There is no sadness here for me
If your happiness I can see

So go my love and don't look back
Make this vigil your very last
This life that God has given you
Take it now and start anew

My memory will live in your heart
For that's the place we are never apart
So live your life, shed no more tears
Then I may rest with no more fears

Gillian Mullett

NATIONAL HYPOCRISY DAY

Out come various medals, the plaudits and awards,
bestowed on all and sundry; not least, for standing tall.
For it's getting near to Remembrance Day,
when hypocrite's, bow their heads to pray,
for those killed in our battles; many miles away.

Flags will fly and trumpets sound,
thousands of poppies will cover the ground.
Pomp and ceremony fill the air
but do little for those who despair;
those men, women and children, who really care.

That in our world there is still poverty to be seen,
women - with young babes in arms, that hungrily scream.
But also there are men with guns and bullets, by the score,
they grin and flaunt their weapons, as they stand by open doors.
Strange, they can afford them, whilst others are so poor.

Who sells, who pays for all these lethal 'toys', weapons
in the hands of many? Some just only boys!
Why it's good old little Britain, providing most of these arms,
at all our countless Arm's Fairs, salesmen deploy their charms
to sell to all and sundry, without the slightest qualms.

So if you've got a few thousand, invest in this vile trade,
then along with our dear old monarch, your fortune too can be made.
Politicians, 'men of brass' all know a thing or two,
as year on year they invest in arms, it's the smartest thing to do.
Remember, there's little worth in human life, just medals for a few!

Peter Mahoney

THE UNKNOWN SOLDIER

Who was he? No one knows!
Somewhere, a mother nursed him,
loved him, watched him grow.
Somewhere, he learned honour,
trust and courage.
Somewhere, he became a man,
strong and proud.
Then somewhere distant, in a far off land,
he gave his all and died, blood seeping
into the soil below.
Later no one knew who he was
but many came to say thank you
for the sacrifice he made and because
their sons did not return.
This, then, may be him,
the son they loved and watched grow.
In this, the tomb of the unknown soldier,
lies a mother's son.

Rose Dempsey

REAL COURAGE

War asks only for death
And as for courage;
It is borne like a cross
After you have buried your prayers for life;
Along with all the faceless dead;
Within your heart is forever but one voice;
That cries out into the wilderness;
Unquenched and unanswered.
'Why?'

Catherine Greenup

SEPTEMBER SONG

'I just called to say I love you.' Stevie Wonder.

Through the limp air
their bodies trip,

like LSD heroics
from a party.

Twenty seconds more
and no return.

The ticker tape
of spent lives

rains down,
anoints the ground.

No superman came flying
as they fell;

no God or gods
rejoicing with their fans.

Hiroshima clouds ‾
corral the streets,

lashing the double-helix
of revenge.

Ashes rise
like incense.

Gerard Rochford

THE TRAIN

Slithers of silk
Eyes glowing in the rancid smell
Of a rotting corpse in the dark

Flies feasting on the s**t of the dead
Then use the brain as a mattress for a bed
Peeking out of one eye with their own
The living embodiment
A beast on a throne

The train, two miles long
Treading unmercifully
The fading sands of time
Looking in the distance
Skeletons and dust
Chained and shackled
Like my master's prize goat

Is the journey nearing the end?
Surely it must be!
The corner's just around the bend
Yes, the journey's at an end

David Chapman

THE MEANING OF WAR

W is for warrior - watchful - waiting
   Weapons - wounding
   Wide-spread - wailing
   Weak (easily broken, bent or defeated)
   Whittle (reduce by repeated subtraction
   Wipe-out - winter
   Windswept - wilderness
   Widow - weeping
   Wondering - why

A is for awful - artillery - arsenal
   Aggressor - assassination
   Anti-personnel - atomise
   Aberration (departure from truth and morality)
   Agony (extreme physical suffering)
   Anybody - anytime
   Anyhow - anywhere
   Aftermath - Airlift
   Abandoned - Absolute

R is for rivers - red - rotting
   Reckless - regardless
   Radioactive - ruin
   Remorseless (acting without compassion)
   Rancour (malignant hatred)
   Recriminations - regrets
   Responsibilities - rights
   Reluctant - reasons
   Rationalisation

Coral Dranfield

HMS ARK ROYAL

She weighs anchor and slips her berth.
Cold grey steel strength, slices ice blue sea
against an ice clear winter sky;
where moon's silver shadow sleeps
and Earth meets with Heaven.

Her stern is laced with white waves
where sun spangles sparkle.
Safely held in the depth of her warmth,
many hands with young beating hearts
speculate they may be sent to war.

A ship has a soul,
Ark Royal's silent
majestic manoeuvres
suggests . . .
she already knows.

Anita Richards

TRENCH BLUES

Of all the things that I despise
   It's the pain I see in my comrade's eyes
His mind is back to before the war
   Of happy times with one and all
His wife and children, mam and dad
   And thinking back it makes him sad
Summer, spring all so good
   But here we are sat in all this mud
This mud that's mixed with comrades dead
   With so much blood it's often red
We often think what it's all for
   This cruel and deadly bloody war
Why all this killing must be done
   The constant shooting, on and on
In this trench he cannot stay
   People dying every day
No ways forward no way back
   Common sense that's what he lacks
Cos if he was bright, a clever mind
   He'd be with the generals far behind
No chance of ever getting shot
   Drinking tea . . . piping hot
Not sat here in this filth and gore
   Fighting a totally pointless war
His eyes once more are full of tears
   Thinking of these wasted years
The things that he will really miss
   His children's squeals his wife's next kiss
His face has changed *this worries me*
   The look of hate yet misery
He leaps to his feet and over the top
   His mind made up he's lived his lot
No more will he just sit and wait
   He's had enough he knows his fate

Gun in hand he starts to run
  As the bullets hit he sees the sun
Hand in hand running in the sea
  Wife and kids, all his family
Seagulls flying way up high
  Drifting in the clear blue sky
No more terror, gore or mess
  He's now at peace . . . true happiness

Bryan Fritchley

REMEMBRANCE DAY - 2003

What do I remember? Whose faces can I recall?
I only remember young faces -
Not grey-haired, dim-eyed or bald.
The faces I knew had a sparkle
The eyes twinkled and mouths that grinned,
Men ready to do their duty
To fight and battle to win

Now sixty years on, we have all changed
(No one would recognise me)
In my head I feel I am young still
But when I look in the glass I can see

So we elderly folk look at faces
To see if there's anything left
Of the young men or women we once knew
But they've all gone - to lie down and rest!

Doris E Pullen

ANCHOR BOOKS
SUBMISSIONS INVITED
SOMETHING FOR EVERYONE

ANCHOR BOOKS GEN - Any subject,
light-hearted clean fun, nothing unprintable
please.

THE OPPOSITE SEX - Have your say on the
opposite gender. Do they drive you mad or can
we co-exist in harmony?

THE NATURAL WORLD - Are we destroying
the world around us? What should we do to
preserve the beauty and the future of our planet -
you decide!

All poems no longer than 30 lines.
Always welcome! No fee!
Plus cash prizes to be won!

Mark your envelope (eg *The Natural World)*
And send to:
Anchor Books
Remus House, Coltsfoot Drive
Peterborough, PE2 9JX

**OVER £10,000 IN POETRY PRIZES
TO BE WON!**

Send an SAE for details on our latest
competition!